To Liam,

This book is dedicated to you, with love and admiration
for the wonderful boy you are becoming
With all my love,
Mami!

RACER'S
GOOD BEHAVIOR ADVENTURES
RACER LEARNS TO USE HIS WORDS

By VIVIANA PEREIRA

In a buzzing town full of brightly colored cars and friendly trucks, lived a little red car named Racer.

One of the things that Racer
loved the most was playing
with his friends and having
a lot of fun.

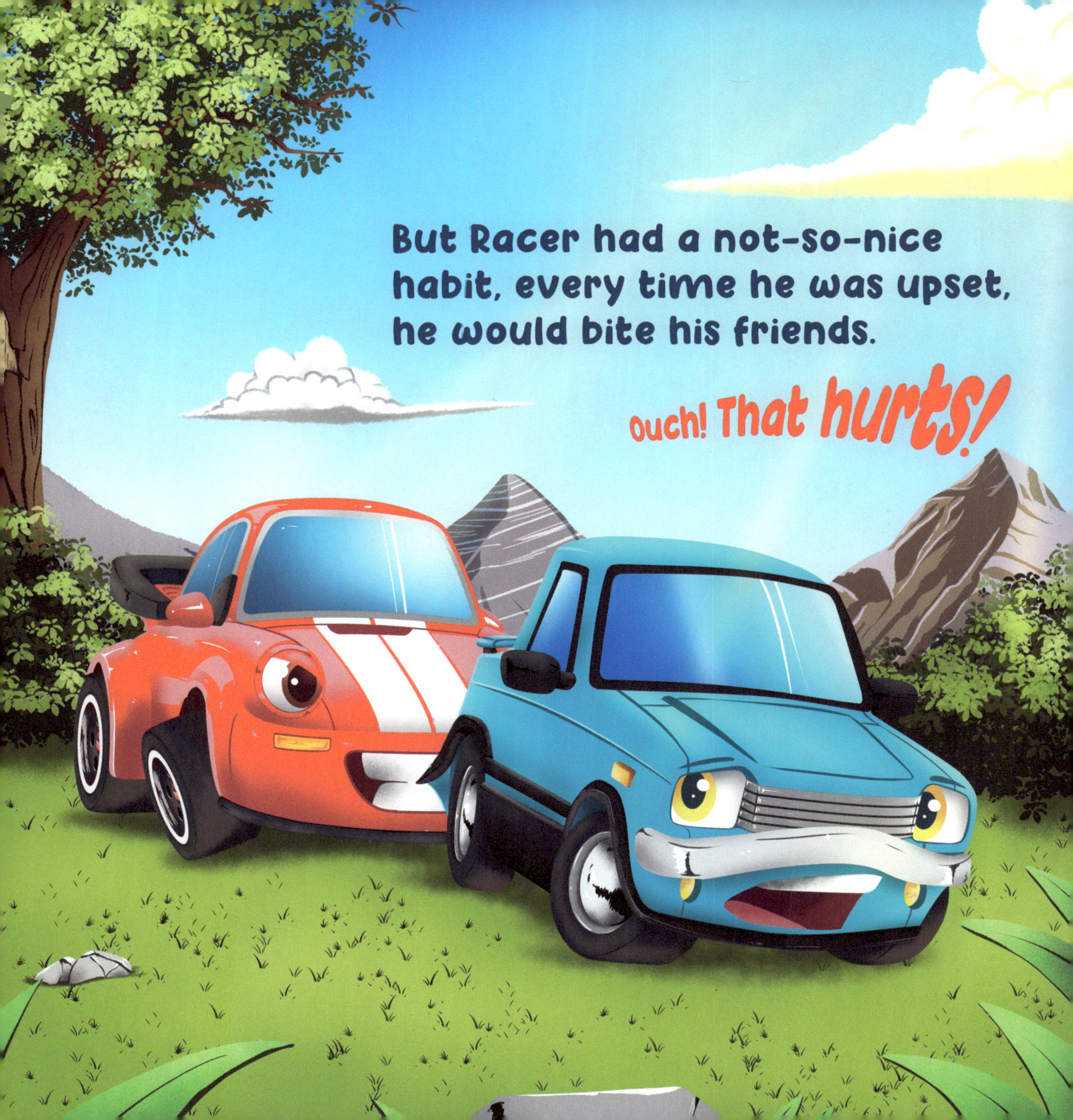

But Racer had a not-so-nice habit, every time he was upset, he would bite his friends.

Ouch! That hurts!

And when Racer bit his friends, they didn't want to play with him anymore because it hurt.

One beautiful, sunny morning,
wise old Grandpa firetruck
visited the town.

He saw Racer get upset
and bite one of his friends.

So, Grandpa assembled all the little
cars and trucks and said,
"Biting is unkind. Instead,
let's try being nice and using
our words"

Racer was confused and asked Grandpa what
he meant. Grandpa explained that
if he bit them, his friends might
not want to play with him as much.

Instead of biting, Grandpa said,
Racer should use his words and say,
'I'M UPSET' or he could ask for help.

Racer decided to try it,
he didn't want to hurt
his friends.

He knew he could use his speed to help them, but could he use his words to express himself rather than hurting them when he was mad?

The next morning, Racer woke up ready to use his words. He was playing ball with his friend the yellow dump truck, Dazzle, but he couldn't keep hold of the ball.

He felt upset and frustrated.
Dazzle was so good at playing
ball, it made him mad.

Now is my chance to try my words,
Racer thought. "I AM UPSET "
Dazzle smiled and said:

"I am Sorry Racer,
how can I help you fell better?
We could play again.
I can show you how I catch?"
Racer grinned

Dazzle helped him catch
and keep the ball and soon
he was really good at it.

Racer felt much better and realized that using his words was nicer than biting.

Racer learned an important
lesson. Biting hurt
his friends and made
them not want to play.

He had a lot of fun and made
more friends by using his words
and being helpful.

All the little cars and trucks learned
that kindness and words were
the key to lasting friendships

THE END